Gifts in the Storm

A Homeless Man's Christmas Story
with accompanying soundtrack

Forrest B. Peterson
Victoria E. King

UNICORN PUBLISHING LLC

Copyright © 2002
by Forrest B. Peterson and Victoria E. King

Illustrations Copyright © 2002
by Victoria E. King

Published by Unicorn Publishing LLC.

To order copies of
"Gifts in the Storm" book and CD,
send a check or money order for
$17.95 + $3.00 S&H for one copy,
for additional books, add $2.00 a copy for S&H
to:
Gifts in the Storm
P.O.Box 700544
St.Cloud, Florida 34770

Also available is the "Gifts in the Storm"
audio book on cassette or CD,
which also comes with the Soundtrack.
$22.95 + $4.00 shipping and handling.

For more information go to
www.giftsinthestorm.com

ISBN: 1-59094-007-5

Gifts in the Storm Soundtrack

Executive Producers: Forrest B. Peterson and
Victoria E. King
Producer: Steve Stack
Associate Producer: Roger Zimish

The following musical selections were composed to correspond with specific themes in the book. The themes are indicated by page numbers, and the selections are referenced in the book with a musical note in the left margin, and a footnote at the bottom of the page. (i.e. Track #1, Winter's Morning.) You will enjoy listening to each rendition as you read the story. The soundtrack may also be enjoyed independently at any time.

1. Gifts in the Storm Prelude   Found on page 9.
Composed and performed by Jenneth Smith.

2. Winter's Morning   Found on page 13.
Composed and performed by Steve Stack.
Copyright 2001. Published by BMI.

3. Concrete Pillow   Found on page 16.
Music and lyrics written by Steve Stack.
Performed by Stacy King.

4. Happy Blues Song   Found on page 21.
Music and lyrics written by Steve Stack.
Performed by Harold Brown, Halie Moyer,
Steven R. Stack, Taylor St.Gordon,
and Dillon St.Gordon.

5. **Someone Who Cares**   Found on page 35.
Music written by Lori Lynn, Roger Zimish,
and Armando Tranquilino.
Lyrics written by Forrest B. Peterson, Lori Lynn
and Roger Zimish.
Performed by Emily Reo.

6. **As Long As There Are Dreams** / Found on page 42.
    Si Puedes Soñar (Mama Rosa's Theme)
Music and lyrics written by A. Del Riego.
Performed by A. Del Riego. Copyright 2002.

7. **The Savior's Star**   Found on page 56.
Music and lyrics written by Lori Lynn.
Performed by Lori Lynn.

8. **Concert for One**   Found on page 59.
    Hallelujah from
      "Christ on Mount of Olives" by Beethoven
    The Little Drummer Boy
    Silent Night
Arranged and accompanied by Guy Vella.
Performed by the Harperville Youth Choir.

9. **Reach Out**   Found on page 71.
Music written by Roger Zimish.
Lyrics written by Forrest B. Peterson and Roger Zimish.
Performed by Roger Zimish and Jenneth Smith.

10. **Cherry Blossoms in the Snow**   Found on page 87.
    (Ode to Mr. Tanaka)
Composed and performed by Guy Vella.

11. **When I Look Into Your Eyes**   Found on page 92.
Music and lyrics written by Steve Stack.
Performed by Steve Stack and Siân Alexandra.

12. **Legacy**   Found on page 96.
Composed by Roger Zimish, Howie Bolton, and Forrest B. Peterson
Performed by Roger Zimish and Howie Bolton.

13. **Gifts in the Storm Reprise**   Found on page 101.
Composed and performed by Jenneth Smith.

Musicians:
Steve Stack: Guitar, keyboard, strings, piano, bass
Roger Zimish: Guitar and keyboard
Howie Bolton: Keyboard
Mike Favata: Percussion
Rich Mueller: Harmonica
A. Del Riego: Guitar
Armando Tranquilino: Keyboard
Guy Vella: Keyboard

Background vocals:
Teri Le, Jennifer Lemons, Lori Lynn, Jenneth Smith, Rebecca Smith, Steve Stack

BIOGRAPHIES:
   Steve Stack is owner/operator of Stack Tracks recording studio in Kissimmee, Florida. He has toured the United States with a variety of bands, including Riot, Basteel, and Thor. He has been writing and performing music for over twenty-five years. He has also been director of music for theater productions throughout central Florida.

Roger Zimish is a music producer and owner/operator of Z Productions, a recording studio in St. Cloud, Florida. He has been writing and producing music since age sixteen, and was a session musician at the Warehouse Jem recording studio in Philadelphia. He has played in a variety of bands, including Lost, High Strung, The Giant Band, Five Kat Jam, and Falcon Taylor Band.

Siân Alexandra was born in Liverpool, England, and has been singing since age 6. She was a featured vocalist at the world famous Arabian Nights Dinner Theater in Orlando. She has also performed at the Wild Bills Dinner Theater in a whip, gun, trick rope, and knife throwing act with her father and brother. As a team they have performed throughout the United Kingdom and the United States.

Howie Bolton is an accomplished musician who plays guitar, piano, and electric bass. He graduated from Los Angeles Valley College, and has played and toured with Clockwise, and Network. He has recently produced and performed on a CD entitled "Free Indeed."

Harold Brown has been performing for over thirty years as a singer. He has appeared at Apollo's Theater and Marla's Place in Los Angeles.

Stacy King is a professional singer and stand up comedian. He produced the TV show "The Underground," and was a performer in the improvisational comedy group called Security Risk.

Lori Lynn is a seventeen year old, who has performed since she was two. Her musical group, Playground, has performed in various places in the United States, including Stratosphere Hotel in Las Vegas. She continues to write and perform her own music.

Emily Reo is thirteen years old, originally from New York, and now living in Orlando. She is studying voice with the acclaimed voice instructor Joann Baker. Emily is a member of the Southwest Show Choir, and has performed in nine Civic Theater plays, including "The Music Man," "Oklahoma," "Scrooge," "Annie," and "Guys and Dolls."

A. Del Riego was born and raised in the Dominican Republic. She has been singing and playing the Spanish guitar for over twenty years. She specializes in traditional boleros. (Romantic Spanish music.) She has recently produced a CD titled "An Gelines." She has performed at Disney World and at a variety of festivals in other parts of the United States. She continues to compose and perform her own music.

Jenneth Smith received her degree in music from Valencia Community College. She is an award winning vocalist. She plays piano and trombone, and also composes her own music.

Guy Vella began playing guitar at age ten, and played in his first band at age thirteen. He studied music at Berklee College. He has released two CD's on MP3.com. He has worked on a variety of projects, including "In Deep," also on MP3.com.

Unicorn Publishing LLC has selected The Ripple Effect Homeless Organization to receive a $1.00 donation from the sale of each Gifts in the Storm Book/CD, which will help support their programs.

The Ripple Effect
"The single act of one touches many."

Founded in 1990, by Kelly Caruso, and based on the philosophy that one person can make a difference, Orlando, Florida's Ripple Effect has grown into a non-profit charity that has touched thousands of lives. Seeking to "restore the self respect of homeless individuals by providing moral and social support through a positive communication network," The Ripple Effect offers services and self-sufficiency tools that enhance long term success.

By creating the opportunity to meet in a safe and pleasant environment, The Ripple Effect brings homeless and non-homeless together. This approach increases the motivation and efficacy levels of the homeless, and increases awareness and volunteer efforts. The Ripple Effect believes that everyone has something valuable to offer, and teaches that free will offers the choice to create a positive or negative wave that touches many. By striving to create a positive ripple effect with your life, The Ripple Effect posits that the tide will bring it right back to you.

For more information about The Ripple Effect, including how you can help make a difference in your community, write to: The Ripple Effect, P.O. Box 990, Orlando, Florida 32802.   www.rippleeffectinfo.org

Gifts in the Storm

A Homeless Man's Christmas Story

Forrest B. Peterson
Victoria E. King

UNICORN PUBLISHING LLC

This book is dedicated to all the homeless people of the world, and to all those who reach out to them with love.

♪ "Are you dead, mister?" The young boy's shout broke the morning silence. He stood at a safe distance, staring at a man's leg protruding from beneath some cardboard and newspapers. There was no movement, but he was ready to run at a moment's warning. He had seen homeless people sleeping next to the garbage containers in Elliot Park before, but not in these freezing temperatures.

Five crows had gathered around, eating bits of scattered food. One bird pecked incessantly at a hole in the man's boot, pulling at his wool sock in search of her morning meal.

The birds flew away as the boy moved closer. He was curious, yet cautious. "Are you dead, mister?" He yelled a little louder.

A muffled voice rumbled from under the cardboard. "I'm not dead yet." The makeshift bedding came alive as the man pushed the newspapers and cardboard away.

Startled by the unexpected reaction, the boy dashed off.

The old, black man struggled to sit up as he watched the little rascal running towards the other side of the park.

The sun reflected off the fresh fallen snow, casting warmth upon the man's face. He squinted against the bright light while pulling away the rest of his bedding. His body trembled. He was cold, but he was more affected by his nightmare; the nightmare that had continued to haunt him for so long. He picked up his harmonica, wiped off the snow and ice, and stuck it in his pocket.

He grabbed the edge of the trash bin, pulled himself up, then slipped on the ice beneath. Catching his balance, he steadied himself against the cold, green metal.

He stood for a moment, soaking up the sun's warmth, trying to defrost his arthritic knees and legs. The pain in his joints kept him at homeless shelters most nights, but last night the weather had caught him off guard. He swung his army-type backpack over his shoulder. It contained his daily accumulations and his poor man's treasures, including three hard backed books, "A Tale of Two Cities," "The Hunchback of Notre Dame," and a Bible, the one given to him by Pastor Franklin. The gold lettering on the front had faded, and duct-tape reinforced the corners. Each page had been read and reread, with his favorite passages marked in colored pencil. Hidden in the front pocket were his steel-rimmed glasses. He had received them from the Lion's Club several years earlier and guarded them well.

Well-worn khaki pants hung loosely around his narrow waist, and he wore a sailor coat with large buttons over his faded, plaid shirt. A frayed scarf wound around his neck and a pullover cap topped his head. His appearance was better than most of the homeless. He was trying to improve.

His name was Cecil. His family name, Martin, had little relevance in the one-name world of the homeless. He had moved quietly among the high-rise buildings in the twin cities of Minneapolis-St.Paul for many years. The homeless were his friends; the old, the teens, the children, as well as a few of the city's more caring fortunate who were willing to reach out. Homelessness was a hard life for anyone, but especially for a seventy-eight-year-old black man having to deal with racial prejudice as well as poverty.

He notices a bottle of Jack Daniels whiskey laying under a bush with enough left for one small drink. He hadn't had a drink in over seven months, but the temptation was still there. It would always be there. Once an alcoholic, always an alcoholic, but that didn't mean that he had to take a drink.

He stared at the enticing black and white label and golden brown liquid. He thought back to his first AA meeting, almost eight months earlier. Standing at the entrance to the meeting room, he looked at the door and then the handle. Turning the knob was the hardest thing he had ever done. It was almost seven o'clock and the meeting was about to start. Almost immediately his fears lessened when two cheerful faces greeted him. "Hello, my name is Kelly, and this is Darryl. Welcome to AA. Please come in."

Cecil moved into the large room, apprehensive but glad he had made it this far. Soon, a man stood, welcomed everyone, and invited those in attendance to share their feelings. Many people stood and spoke about their experiences with alcohol. The meeting went on for an hour or so. Cecil was sitting in the back listening intently touched by their words. He had always been hesitant to express his feelings and he didn't want to speak, but something tugged at his heart and he finally stood. He approached the podium slowly.

"Hello, my name is Cecil."

"Hello, Cecil," the group responded in unison.

"I'm an alcoholic, and I want to change. Many years ago, my family and I were in a serious automobile accident. . ."

He was brought back to the moment as hunger pains shot through his stomach. He pulled out a half eaten bologna sandwich and nibbled at his breakfast while making his way across the park in the ankle-high snow. The park was quiet and wrapped in a thick, white blanket. The harsh surface of the city had been softened overnight.

Cecil was a former professor whose heartbreaks of the past continued to pull him into a life of guilt and despair. He was striving to change his forty years of homelessness and self-condemnation to a happier way of life, and the past eight months had brought new direction. He had become friends with three white children, Angela, Jackie, and Sue Beth, the children who called him Grandpa Cecil. He had met them at a homeless shelter, the Macaby House, and visited with them as much as possible. The shelter was founded by Sarah Macaby and her late husband, Marshall, and for almost ten years Sarah had put her wealth into the home. She had always seen in Cecil a potential for change, and now, after all these years, she was thrilled that his motivation was returning.

♪ Cecil stopped for a moment in awe of the glistening trees throughout the park. The pines were covered in a thick layer of sparkling icicles that dangled from the branches, putting unusual weight on the fragile limbs. He studied them with the interest of an art critic, appreciating nature's creative genius. The sun reflected off the crystals, displaying the perfect Christmas trees. As a light breeze passed over the icicles, a tinkling sound arose like bells ringing in the holidays.

Movement from the street caught his attention as two people exited a large van. A man and a woman carrying a video camera and other equipment marched quickly in his direction. He shied away, attempting to keep his distance.

"Hey! Wait a minute!" The lady caught up with him. "I'm Nancy Adams with WKRX News Center Ten. We are doing a Christmas Eve special on how the homeless spend their Christmas Holiday."

"I don't really have anything to say." Cecil turned.

"It will only take a minute," she pushed. "What's your name?"

He paused and resisted, he was a private person. "Cecil."

"And your last name?"

"My name is Cecil. How do you know I'm homeless?"

"We noticed you sleeping over there. . ." She pointed towards the garbage cans.

Cecil raised an eyebrow. "Maybe I like sleeping in the snow."

Shrugging off his answer she continued, "If you'll help out with the interview, I have a couple of coupons for Burger King. You know; a hamburger and fries."

The food sounded nice, but even more importantly he could talk about the Macaby Homeless shelter; a place that had helped him so much over the years. "Okay, I will do your interview."

"That's great. Stand right here and don't be nervous," she said as she checked her makeup.

The camera man adjusted the tripod, while directing Cecil, "Look at the reporter, not the camera." He lowered his voice. "Now, Nancy, remember; be kind! Okay, we are ready, -three, two, one." With a pointed finger, he signaled the reporter to begin.

"This is Nancy Adams with WKRX TV. Today we are looking at the increasing problems of the homeless and the holidays. Over three million homeless people are spread across the nation, with several thousand in our own city. The homeless are spending their Christmas on the streets, in cars, in abandoned buildings, in freight trains, and on the river front. I am here talking with Cecil." She turned to Cecil, took his arm, and pulled him closer to the camera. "Today is Christmas Eve. How are you going to spend the day?

She pointed the microphone at Cecil and he hesitated again. Finally he answered, "I have special places and special people that I visit, and this evening I will be at the Macaby house for dinner with my friends. The Macaby House is a wonderful organization that helps the homeless. It was founded nine years ago by Marshall and Sarah Macaby. Sarah is a very nice lady, who . . ."

"That's great. When did you become homeless?"

"Why do you want to know that?"

Her smile tightened, as she pressed on, "There is a major storm coming in later today. How do the homeless deal with extreme weather conditions?"

"Well, unfortunately, too many of my friends will be spending Christmas on the street; not enough shelters to go around, but I'm spending the night at the Macaby House."

"I understand that most homeless people are either

mentally ill, alcoholics, or drug abusers. Is that true?" she asked.

"Some are. . . but it's not that simple."

"Is it true that tragedies in life can pull a person into homelessness?"

"I thought you wanted to talk about Christmas!"

"What caused you to become homeless?" She pushed even harder.

Cecil's body went rigid, and knots tightened in his stomach. He said quietly, "I would rather not talk about it. I have no more to say! I really need to go!" He turned and started walking down the path.

"Hey, you forgot your coupons."

He kept moving, not looking back.

"Did I say something wrong?" she asked the cameraman.

"I've told you before, Nancy, you can't treat people like that and expect them to cooperate."

♪ Cecil hurt deep inside. Old wounds had been ripped open again. He approached a park bench, brushed off the snow, and fell back on the hard wooden slates, trying to control his emotions.

"What does she know about tragedy?" He put his hands over his face. Visions of the past darted around in his head; snow flakes smashing against the windshield, the deer in the road, the car sinking in the water. He hit his head with his fists, increasing the intensity as he tried to beat out the memories. But the yells and screams from that tragic night continued to haunt him and the guilt remained.

"And what does she know about drinking and the homeless?" He struggled to regain his composure, remembering that today was supposed to be special. It was Christmas Eve, and more so than any other day, Cecil reached into the depth of his soul and extracted the most positive elements of his being. He wanted this day to be filled with positive feelings and events, for this was his poor man's journey of joy.

Since he arrived in the twin cities eighteen years earlier, he had enjoyed a Christmas Eve ritual. Visiting special places and friends fulfilled his personal holiday celebration. But this year he had an additional goal. For several months he had prayed, meditated, and searched the scriptures. He felt that God had forgiven him but now he needed to forgive himself and release the guilt. This was the day to fulfill that goal. He stood with a renewed determination to make this a great day. By the time he reached the other side of the park, much of the grief had lifted.

His attention was drawn to a group of boys placing the finishing touches on a snowman that stood over five feet tall. Huge balls of snow made up his three-tiered anatomy. The children had placed some rocks for his eyes and a stick for his mouth but were lacking something distinctive for their new friend's nose.

Something that would magically transform their creation into an animated Frosty the Snowman.

The smallest boy spotted Cecil, recognizing him as the man who had been lying in the snow. He shifted closer to his friends. "Check your pockets guys. We need something for the nose, something really cool. Something magical."

"Yeah, right," said a nine-year-old who was far too pragmatic for his age, a state of mind that poured cold water, and sometimes cold snow, on too many of his friends' imaginary endeavors. The kids began rummaging through their pockets.

The search was in full swing when a fun-loving prankster pulled out a banana and quickly shoved the end into the center of the snowman's face. He grinned mischievously. "There, now he's perfect."

Everyone laughed except for Mr. Pragmatic who stared in contempt. "It looks like an arctic toucan. All we need now is to add some feathers."

Cecil watched intently. Then, without thinking, he reached to the bottom of his coat and tore off one of the big buttons. As Cecil came nearer, he noticed the little rascal hiding behind a bigger boy, and gave him a little wink. He stretched out his gloved hand. "How would this be for a nose?"

The boys looked up. They were a bit startled and somewhat apprehensive but their attention was drawn to Cecil's hand bearing the button nose gift.

"That's perfect, mister."

"Best nose I've ever seen."

"Much better than that dumb banana."

"Well, it's yours if you want it," Cecil said.

One of the older boys reach out and cautiously remove the button from Cecil's hand. The boy's faces beamed as he pulled out the banana and pushed in the button. As he pushed it deeper into the snow, the boys held their breath in anticipation, hoping that the snowman might magically come to life. But there he stood in all his white, glittering glory, –motionless.

With a little sigh, the youngest broke the silence, "Well, at least he's really cool."

"Boys, I must move on. I have many things to do and see today. Merry Christmas!"

"Merry Christmas! Thanks for the button." the boys responded, as they started packing snow tightly in their hands.

Cecil had only taken a few steps when the scene behind him exploded into a snowball fight.

The late morning was bright but still cold enough for the snow to remain, even in the busy down town. The vigorous walking was warming Cecil, and finally thawing out his toes and loosening his joints.

Across Park Avenue, Cecil spotted a group of children ice skating on a small rink. Their laughter reminded him of Angela, Jackie, and Sue Beth. The children and their mother, Linda Matthews, had recently joined the ranks of the homeless. Their husband and father had died of a heart attack. Linda could only regret that they had no savings and no insurance. Cecil reflected upon the day they arrived at the Macaby House.

He recalled how shy and aloof the children had been at first and how unfriendly he must have seemed in his grimy clothes and ragged condition. Then suddenly one day, as Cecil completed his dinner, he sat back, fished out his harmonica, and began to play. Angela was instantly drawn to the music and slowly moved into the dining room with the two younger children close behind.

Cecil raised his eyes over the edge of his steel rimmed glasses. Before him stood three freckled-faced towheads.

"Now, what can I do for you beautiful children?" he said, as he took his glasses off and stuck them in the pocket of his dirty shirt.

"I'm not beautiful," Jackie said firmly. "I'm a boy, and boys are handsome."

"And so you are."

Sue Beth peaked at Cecil from behind Angela, and asked, "Am I beautiful too?"

Cecil bent over and looked into her timid face, "Someday you could be Miss America."

"My name is Angela, and this is my brother and sister, Jackie and Sue Beth."

"It's nice to meet you," Cecil said.

"What were you playing?" Sue Beth interrupted.

"It's the blues. My Grandpa Joshua taught me how to play. He was from Baton Rouge, in Louisiana, and played in a jazz band."

"The blues? It sounds sad," said Angela.

"The blues can be sad, but it can also be very happy."

"I'd like to hear a happy, blue song, please?" Jackie requested.

♪   "I'll tell you what, I'm going to make up a song just for the three of you. We'll call it. . . " he paused, looked at the children, and said with a smile. ". . .*The Happy Blues Song.*"

Cecil began playing different blues chords, searching for the right sound and rhythm. He cupped his hands around the harmonica, tapped his foot, and soon the song was born. He played the cheerful music while the children clapped to the beat. He lowered the harmonica and began to sing, ending each sentence with a few more chords.

"There were three little kids sitting next to me. They said, hey, won't you play a song. Please, something happy, something fun, something old, something new." He continued playing and singing, and concluded with, "We'll sing a happy, happy, blues song. The kind of song we can all sing along." The children joined in the chorus as Cecil played the harmonica, and they sang and sang until Cecil was totally out of breath.

"Let's make up another song," Jackie blurted out.

Cecil gulped, and rolled his eyes, "How about we make up another song tomorrow? We'll call it; Lets sing a blues song until we're all out of breath and can't sing anymore-song."

"Yeah, that's a great song!"

The four of them sat there for quite a while, getting to know each other better. They laughed, told stories, and enjoyed each others company.

Angela looked closely at Cecil's face, her bright blue eyes sparkled and reflected a maturity far beyond her ten years of age. She was the oldest of the three children, and had taken on many parental responsibilities. Some of these duties were by her mother's request, while others were self appointed.

"Your face looks like a map," she said as she

reached up, softly touching the lines and age marks on his face.

He thought for a moment. "In many ways they are like roads on a map. They are my roads. My wrinkles are the journeys of my life."

Their mother's voice broke the special moment, beckoning their return. The three children responded instantly, running off toward the recreation room. Angela stopped at the doorway, looked back, and smiled a little, as she watched the old man searching for his glasses.

"They're in your shirt pocket," she said. "What's your name mister-music-man?"

He turned towards the cheery voice. "Cecil."

Her smile widened. "See you later, grandpa Cecil. Have a nice day."

The bark of a scroungy, old mutt brought Cecil back to reality. Wandering through the heart of the city, he passed by buildings of every design, shape and size, which intimidated his five-foot-ten-inch frame. He had always felt insignificant beneath the dominance of the massive structures. Still, the starkness of the city could not overshadow the festive feelings of the Holiday and his excitement of fulfilling his goal.

Cecil travelled for a block or so, when he heard a familiar sound. Standing under an awning next to the Twin City Coffee Shop, was his friend Danny Boy. He was playing a Christmas song on his guitar and singing along, in hopes that the busy shoppers would appreciate his efforts and make a donation. As Cecil drew closer, he noticed that Danny's eyes were closed, being emotionally connected to the song. Cecil appreciated Danny's talents. They had often jammed together.

Danny had gone to the streets in search of meaning, as he put it. He came from a wealthy background and had done doing well in school. Then, in his junior year in college, he dropped out. His desire to gain an education, to gain more wealth, turned into cynicism for a world too full of inequality. He had been on the streets for almost eighteen months. Cecil watched him intently. How much he loved this young man, so smart, so concerned, and so lost. He looked at his long auburn hair and beard and thought how Danny could have looked like Jesus. The only thing out of place was his leather western hat, sun glasses, denim jacket, and a peace sign necklace.

The song ended, and Danny immediately looked in his guitar case to see if he was going to eat today, but then he noticed Cecil.

"Hey, man, wuz up? I was hoping to see you before Christmas. I have some good news. Do you have time for some coffee? I have a few bucks here. I guess someone likes my singing, or is it just the season?" he continued to rattle on.

They entered the coffee shop, and looks from all directions came their way. A waitress approached their booth, and just stood there without saying a word.

"Two coffees, please, black."

She stopped chewing her gum. "Do you have any money?"

Danny and Cecil didn't say a word, they simply looked at each other. Danny pulled out a couple dollars, and placed them on the table.

She raised her eyebrows, and moved away.

"How are you doing, Danny Boy?"

"I'm doing okay. The nights get cold, but do I need to tell you about that? I've been staying with some friends down by the river. I make enough from my singing to get by, especially during the holidays. People are more giving."

"How are your parents doing?" Cecil asked.

"Oh, I think they're understanding better where I'm coming from. That brings me to what I wanted to tell you. This is going to be my Christmas present to you. You know how you've been trying to get me off the street and back to school?"

Cecil nodded and smiled.

"Well, that's what I'm going to do. I'm going to study social work. Being on the street has shown me that what's important in the world are people. Isn't that what life's all about? Helping people?"

"Danny Boy, I think you have found what you've been looking for."

"You think so?"

"Yes, you have found a purpose, and you couldn't have given me a greater gift."

"I'm flying home tomorrow. My parents and I have some things to talk over, you know, some fences to mend. I'll start school in January, but I'm not going back to Dartmouth. I'm going to a little school in Montana."

"God bless you, Danny, and be good to yourself."

"By the way, how are the kids doing?"

"Well, they will be getting a place of their own soon. Jackie still thinks he's the boss, Sue Beth is still shy, but she's coming out of her shell, and Angela, I tell ya,' she's one brave little girl. She takes on a lot of responsibility for someone her age. You know, Danny, each day they're becoming more and more a part of me. I love them so much."

"I'm sure they love you too. Getting a home of their own is going to mean a lot to them. Now, how about you Cecil, isn't this your big day? I know you have been preparing quite a while for this," Danny said, as he took a sip of his coffee.

"I'm ready to let go, but the past is difficult to surrender."

"I know what happened to your family,. . . their death,. . . he contemplated for a moment, . . . some things just happen."

"I wish I was as certain as you are. Giving up the guilt and the pain is the hardest thing I've ever tried to do. But for some reason, deep down in my soul, I feel that there is something out there that I'll find, something that will bring this to an end. I need to do this for the children and for my family.

"And don't forget yourself," Danny said, "Cecil, I'm not a religious person, but I'm going to say a prayer for you today."

They exited the cafe and embraced.

The waitress returned to the table and found the money for the coffee. She noticed something written on a napkin; Merry Christmas from Cecil and Danny. Under the napkin was a five dollar bill. She looked out the window and watched the two men part in opposite directions. Tears filled her eyes as she whispered, "I'm sorry, and Merry Christmas to you."

Cecil soon arrived at the first stop on his journey, The Rankin department store, one of the city's most elite establishments and Marshall-Fields' major competition. He meandered through the store, taking in the warmth and the holiday decorations. The aroma of popcorn, candy, perfume, and leather intermixed to create the department-store smell and atmosphere. He pretended that this was his house, all decorated with thousands of dollar's worth of white, snow-flocked trees, adorned with large, silver bulbs and metallic blue garland.

In the center of the first floor, suspended from the ceiling, was an enormous Santa sleigh. Cecil stopped to examine it closer. It was being pulled by eight reindeer and led by Rudolph with his red nose flashing. At the back of the sleigh were three elves hanging onto the runners for dear life, while Santa sat securely inside. The whole succession appeared to zoom across the sky. All of this magnificent holiday adventure was brought to life by synchronized robotics.

The aisles were crowded with last-minute shoppers grabbing this and that and hurrying to complete their Christmas lists. Cecil walked among the candy counters with rows and rows of gourmet chocolates, hard candies, and many European treats such as marzipan, Leckerli, and Kipfel.

As he stepped around yet another counter, his eyes

fell upon a glass showcase, heaped with his favorite confection; handmade, milk chocolate fudge. He stared at the case for a few moments. The sales person behind the counter noticed Cecil. She was wearing a festive green and red elf outfit, topped with a Santa hat. Her gold name tag prominently stated that she was Santa's Helper. Cecil reached into his pocket and pulled out all his money. He had a quarter and a dime. The sign on the fudge section declared; Gourmet Fudge, made with real butter and cream, $28 per pound.

The clerk looked at Cecil's hand, and saw the money. "Sir, would you like some fudge?"

Cecil looked at the two coins in his hand, then the candy, and then the sales sign again, but his discouraging thoughts were interrupted by the smiling face behind the counter.

"Sir, the fudge is on sale right now. Several pieces for thirty cents plus tax. It would be thirty-two cents total."

Cecil's mind was not as sharp as it used to be, but he understood what she was doing and he was grateful. He handed her the money and waited patiently for her to fill the little bag.

"Thank You! Merry Christmas," he said, as she handed him the change and the white bag embellished with glittering, silver snowflakes. He looked from the bag to her kind face and said, "You really are Santa's helper!"

She broke into a radiant smile.

Soon, a Rankin security officer was following Cecil, scrutinizing his every move. He was new with the Rankin store, a police officer fresh from the academy, doing part-time work as a security guard.

Cecil went directly to the elevator and pushed the 'up' button. His next stop was Santa Land. The doors opened and revealed a crowded compartment. He moved in, leaving barely enough room for the doors to close behind him. Several of the people looked in his direction. Disdain, if not disgust, was evident on their sanctimonious faces. A well-dressed lady in a fur coat stood next to Cecil. She tried to gain some distance from him, but had no room to move. She pulled a perfumed handkerchief from her pocket, and held it to her nose. She looked over at Cecil with raised eyebrows, coughed a few times, and tried hard to inform everyone of her displeasure.

The elevator passed the fourth, fifth, and sixth floor, as the operator announced each stop with the eloquence of an English butler.

"Seventh floor. Men's wear, shoes, coats, and ties."

The lady waited impatiently.

"Eighth floor. Children's wear and toys,"

The doors opened, and Cecil stepped out.

The lady removed her handkerchief. "It seems that a store of this quality would not allow filthy people like that to roam around."

Cecil turned, and slightly bowed, "My dear madam,

Happy Holidays to you, and may your desires for mankind be returned to you a hundred-fold."

Close to the elevator was the entrance to one of Rankin's most magnificent creations; Santa's Workshop. The spacious log cabin was decorated in bright colors with intricate ornamentation. Beautiful icicle lights hung from the eaves and the warm glow of candlelight glimmered in the frosted windows. As Cecil walked through the door, he felt the magic penetrating his entire being. He was greeted by several elves, little people attired in lavish costumes rivaling those in the "Wizard of Oz" movie.

"Welcome to Santa's Workshop. My name is Herman. I am head elf. Follow me, please."

Cecil looked around the elaborate workshop, and saw more than a dozen elves busy at work. Some were real, while others were mechanical. At the far end of the workshop, Santa was sitting on a large, gold throne with a huge, carved back and a blue velvet seat-cushion. He visited with each child as they came through a long line, all of them waiting in anticipation. Some of the children were more patient than others.

Rankin's Santa was like no other. His burgundy-red suit was trimmed with simulated gray fox fur, and the massive leather boots were knee high. Handcrafted leather straps with large, brass bells were draped on the front and back of the suit, and were attached to a wide belt that wrapped around Santa's chubby belly. He was a combination of the modern and the old world Santa. His pure white beard and hair were real, and perfectly manicured.

One by one, children from different backgrounds and cultures sat upon Santa's lap, confiding their wishes, hopes, and dreams. All were accepted unconditionally. Cecil thought how wonderful it would be if everyone in the world could be as accepting as Santa.

Soon a small girl was perched upon his lap. Her dark eyes sparkled as she spoke boldly. She gestured with her hands and expressed her deepest wishes for the holiday season. She reminded him of his own daughter, with black curls framing an ebony face.

"I want a doll that talks, a stove that bakes cakes, and a Barbie doll computer. Not a play one, but a real one," she said with complete expectation.

Cecil listened intently. Only a little child can be so clear-minded and trusting, he thought. He had come to realize that it was simple moments like these that were, in reality, the most profound.

The little girl jumped down from Santa's lap, and noticed Cecil standing off to the side. She walked up to him and said directly, "Hi, my name is Darla Marie Crawford, and I'm five years old. What is your name?"

"Cecil."

"How old are you?" she asked in her uninhibited manner.

"Too old."

"My daddy plays for the Timberwolves, and I live on Lake of the Isle Boulevard. It's on the hill. Where do you live?"

Cecil paused, and looked around, as if he was searching for a place to call his own. Finally, he bent over and looked into Darla's eyes. "The world is my home. I live everywhere."

At that moment the security officer interrupted, and took Darla by the hand.

"Your mother is looking for you." His stare was directed at Cecil.

"It's okay mister," Darla declared. "Cecil is a nice man."

"You need to leave the store!" the security officer said. "I'll call the the police if you don't. You don't want to spend Christmas in jail do you?"

Cecil turned, and walked down the aisle. He did not want to cause any problems. He looked back and saw his new, little friend standing next to one of the toy counters with her mother.

Darla waved and called out, "Merry Christmas! Happy New Year!"

Cecil returned the gesture, and gave her a big smile. As he continued to walk, he shook his head as if to clear his mind of the memories; memories that were too bittersweet and painful. Then he remembered his goal to let go of the pain.

Angela climbed on board the Macaby House van and sat down behind the driver. Terry sat down next to her. He was a dark-haired, green eyed boy she had met several months earlier. He must never find out that she has a crush on him. The van was full with about twenty children, and several parent chaperones. Angela looked at Jackie and Sue Beth, who were sitting towards the back. She waved and smiled, "Don't forget your seat belts." The van pulled out and started down the road.

Terry turned to Angela and asked, "Where is this place we're going to?"

"Mrs. Macaby told me that the Shriners have a party for the Macaby House children every year."

"What are Shriners?"

"They are rich old men who dress up like clowns, and ride motor scooters, at least that's what they do in parades. They also do nice things for children," Angela said.

"My mother told me something about getting clothes," Terry stated.

"After the party, we'll all go to a big store, and they'll buy us new clothes and toys."

"They sound like really nice people."

"Oh, they are! Helping people is their hobby." Angela looked back to make sure that Jackie and Sue

Beth had buckled their seat belts. She glanced out the window, looked up and down the streets, "I wonder where Grandpa Cecil is?" she questioned out loud.

"Why do you call him grandpa?" Terry asked. "He can't be your grandpa, he's black."

♪ Angela's eyebrows raised as she looked directly at Terry, "Oh, I really hadn't noticed." She turned back to the window and reflected with excitement the Macaby House Christmas Eve dinner, and that Cecil would be there with them. He had promised to play all her favorite Christmas songs on his harmonica.

Sarah and Linda had remained at the house, cleaning and preparing for the dinner party. Sarah was taking a short lunch break and was making a peanut butter sandwich in the kitchen when Linda entered.

"Would you like a sandwich?" Sarah asked.

"No thank you, I had a late breakfast." Linda placed the broom and dustpan in the utility closet. "I have discovered one thing though; this place is much easier to clean without twenty little bodies running around."

"But what a joy they are! And I miss them when they're gone," Sarah said. "You know, Linda, it was children like yours that motivated my husband and me to establish the Macaby House. Marshall was a good man. He was a senator for many years and a successful business man. We established this home about a year before he died. That was ten years ago now. I was never able to have children, but the children here at the home have filled that void."

"How did your husband die?" Linda asked.

"Smoking! Unfortunately he was a chain smoker and died of lung cancer."

"That must have been difficult."

"Yes, it was. We loved each other very much. He was an honest man. He legislated many programs that benefitted young people, and also the homeless, of course."

"Sarah, I want to thank you for allowing us to be here at the Macaby House. Your love and support is truly appreciated. When Frank died, I didn't know what to do. We didn't have family to turn to, so we stayed at several shelters in New York City where we lived at the time. But they had little to offer. We were thrilled when a friend told us about your home and excited when you invited us to stay. The way you work with people is wonderful; helping them get back on their feet, and helping them gain their independence. The children feel secure here. The love they have received from you and Cecil, and other residents too, has meant so much to them."

"Yes, the children and Cecil have been good for each other. Cecil has improved a lot. He has given up his drinking, and has been attending AA meetings regularly. He is trying to do better."

"There was a time, right after Frank's death, when

the kids just gave up. Did you know that at one time Angela was in a gifted program in school? It wasn't until Cecil entered their lives that their motivation returned. Good grief, look at the time. If we go on blabbing like this, we'll never get the house clean."

Sarah looked at her untouched sandwich, and smiled to herself.

About an hour later, the van pulled into the driveway, and soon the house was active and noisy again. Angela, Jackie, and Sue Beth stood before their mother, donned in new outfits and big grins.

"Wow, you guys look great!"

Jackie turned around, to show off his new back pack, so Sue Beth had to do the same to show her new hair clip.

Linda laughed, then asked, "How was the party?"

"Oh, the party and the shopping were fun, but something was really strange." Angela threw her hands in the air. "Not all the Shriners were old, only two of them were clowns, and I didn't even see one motor scooter."

The snow began falling again, and Cecil watched the large, fluffy flakes accumulate all around him. They gently settled like white, flowing angels, selecting their path of descent to ultimately find their special places on earth .

Before long, he arrived at the Mulholland Bakery. He paused in front of the large window which was frosted and brightly painted with holly around the edge. The smell of fresh, hot pastries seemed to permeate the entire street. His stomach churned in anticipation of something to eat, but his attention was drawn to a beautiful mini-town in the center of the window. Nestled in frosting snow, was row upon row of brightly decorated gingerbread houses. Asphalt streets made of flattened licorice lay in a crisscross pattern throughout the town. Small cars, street signs, and people were strategically placed to create this festive illusion. Gumdrop trees and Lifesaver wreaths trimmed the scene in green and red. Toy children and a little dog skated on an ice rink made from the magic of a pastry chef's glaze, and a small electric train encircled the town.

Looking upon the scene, he reminisced about his own childhood, a childhood that was not much different from the vision that lay before him. His concentration was transformed into a semi-hypnotic state as he watched the miniature train continuously circle the tracks.

His thoughts went back in time, drawing from the archives of his mind. Almost as if it was yesterday, memories of a special Christmas flowed through him.

The year was 1930 and Cecil was seven years old, living on the outskirts of Philadelphia, Pennsylvania. His parents had a little dairy farm which provided a meager but secure living. Life was challenging at the onset of the depression, especially for a black family. Cecil was the second to the youngest of the children. Each Christmas morning, as part of their family tradition, he and his four brothers and sisters gathered with their parents and Grandpa Joshua around the potbelly stove. Father would first read the Christmas story from the Book of Luke, and the children knew it would be time to open their gifts as soon as he had finished.

Cecil had heard the story many times before, but each time the power of the message still awakened his faculties. He was especially touched when Mary and Joseph were told that there was no room at the inn. The children would sit in an emotional dilemma, as they wanted to enjoy the story, but also wanted to open their presents. Father would finish the account by relating how Santa, due to fog, almost missed coming to their house. Then everyone would dash to the tree.

"Now remember," mother instructed, as she did every year, "unwrap your gifts carefully, so we can save the paper."

Mother was so frugal, she made penny pinchers

look frivolous. But they respected her request, preserved each sheet, and folded it up nicely. They understood that times were hard.

Cecil received his Christmas wish, a World War I biplane, fashioned after the famous German Red Baron's aircraft. Like most of their gifts, it was handmade. Father had spent many hours hand-crafting the plane from a picture in a magazine. He was good with his hands and made most of the children's gifts. He could make anything from airplanes to dolls.

He received another special gift that year. Grandpa Joshua gave him his first harmonica, an M. Hohner Marine Band model. For the next several months the incessant practice drove his family crazy, until his skills improved. And from that time on, music became an important part of his life.

As he was fondly reminiscing, Mrs. Abernathy, the bakery owner, tapped on the glass and peered through the icy panes. She was bent over the mini town, looking like Gulliver invading Lilliput. She gave him a holiday smile that was big enough to fill any heart. He returned the gesture with a wide grin and a hearty wave. Mrs. Abernathy reached out to the less fortunate. Her heart was in the right place. She disappeared, and a moment later came bounding out the door, gracefully carrying her large roly-poly frame. Her white uniform was stained profusely with cherry, blueberry, lemon, and orange frosting. She was working diligently to finish the last of her pastry orders.

"Cecil, at last! Where have you been? I've been waiting for you," she said in her slight Norwegian accent. "Come in and warm your bones. You're looking good, ja! It's nice to see that you're doing so much better."

She took him by the arm and guided him into the store where the sweet smell was even more intense. She continued the non-stop chatter.

"Merry Christmas to you. How have you been?" she asked, as she handed him a bag of warm, fresh goodies. The bag most certainly included Cecil's favorite; raspberry Bismarks.

"Do you have a place to stay tonight?" she asked with concern. "I have a bed in the back of the store if you would like to stay the night."

"Thank you very much. You are so kind, but I must make it to the Macaby House so I can spend Christmas with my little friends."

"You better hurry then. I heard on the radio that a big cold front is moving in later this evening."

Cecil thanked her for the pastries and the information, then reluctantly opened the door to continue his journey, wishing he could take a bundle of warm air with him. He looked up at the mammoth clock perched atop the Union Pacific railroad station. He wanted to complete his Christmas ritual, but he also knew it was imperative that he make it to the Macaby House before the storm reached full force.

Cecil was excited about his next stop; the garbage bins at the Imperial Porcelain Company. From time to time he had found beautiful, hand-painted figurines of little Dutch girls, matadors, Chinese dancers, and others. Sometimes one of the works would be in good condition, but most often they would have a few chips or cracks. He was hoping to find gifts for the children. It had been a long time since Cecil had even thought about giving someone a present, but this year he wanted to give each of the children something special.

He moved along, street after street, corner after corner, heading for the Porcelain Company. He turned at the end of the block, and noticed a familiar face about halfway down the street. She was an elderly, Mexican woman everyone called Mama Rosa. Her real name was too hard to pronounce, at least for gringos. She was pushing a shopping cart half-full of her daily collection of aluminum cans, a broken toaster, bottles and newspapers, wares she could sell as salvage.

Mama was a thin, frail woman with a face of brown, wrinkled skin. She was mostly toothless but still possessed a smile, a lonely smile, but still a smile. She had wanted to return to El Paso, Texas for many years, but ♪ it was just a dream.

Cecil caught up with her, and she turned toward him, "Cecil, where are you been? No see for long

♪ 6. **As Long As There Are Dreams**

time." Not waiting for an answer, she continued, "You hear Major Moore and Terry was found muerto, dead, in tunnel?"

The Major had also been a homeless man. Mentally ill but harmless. He held delusions of grandeur, and fancied himself a Civil War Major and hero. His son Terry, also troubled, had served as his attaché.

"They freezed in their sleep. Very sad. Dios Bendigalo."

"I'm sorry to hear that. They were nice people. It's a hard world out there." He sighed, but then thought of something, "Mama, do you have plans for Christmas?"

"I meet some amigos. We go to Salvation Army for dinner."

Cecil reached over and gave her a hug. "Mama Rosa, you be good to yourself, okay? Have a Merry Christmas, Senora, and a great New Year."

"Muchos gracias. Feliz Navidad," she said, as she struggled to push the cart down the slippery, ice covered sidewalk. Cecil paused and watched her old body shuffle along. He felt sad because of the way Mama had to live her life, forgetting for a moment that his condition was not all that different from Mama Rosa's. As Cecil continued on, he thought about Major Moore and Terry, friends who were no longer part of his homeless family.

The temperature was slowly dropping, and the cold was depleting Cecil's energy. He leaned against a brick building, reached into the paper bag, and took a big bite of the chilled, but still delicious Bismarck. The raspberry filling dripped down the side of his mouth as his attention was drawn to bright lights on one of the city's main boulevards. Cecil looked closer and discovered that the long avenue was trimmed in an entire holiday theme. Telephone poles, decorated like candy canes, lined the sidewalks, and gold and red garland stretched across each intersection with luminous angels suspended majestically in the middle of each. They reminded him of his own little angels; Angela, Jackie, and Sue Beth.

He recalled, only a few weeks earlier, when he had found Angela sitting in the stairs at the Macaby House. Her head was buried in her arms, and she was sobbing like she had lost her most prized possession.

Cecil had approached her and asked softly, "Angela, what's the matter?"

He sat down beside her and placed his arm around her shoulders. "Please talk to me Angela. Your grandpa can't help you if you won't talk, now can he?"

She looked up as tears rolled down her pale cheeks.

"How can anything be that bad?" he asked.

Angela wiped away her tears with the back of her

hand, but the pain remained.

"Now let me see an Angela-angel smile," he encouraged. A tiny smile appeared, reflecting more her appreciation for his concern than any relief from her emotional turmoil.

"Tell me what is troubling you," he persisted.

She thought for a while. Then, like an exploding pressure cooker, she shouted, "I hate what I am! Homeless, white trash! I hate it!"

Cecil waited, trying to hitch his wagon-load of experience to the need of the moment.

"Who told you that?"

"People," she said.

"What people?"

"Kid people!" Again tears filled her eyes. "That awful Henry! Steve! And Allison too! They said homeless people like me are white trash. I hate them!"

He thought for a few moments. "Even if some people say unkind words, it doesn't mean that what they say is true. Do you believe that?"

"I don't know."

"It doesn't matter whether you live in a mansion or in a hut, whether you are a queen or a little girl, what matters is what is in your heart. We need to love the world as God loves us, unconditionally. Some people will choose to bury that love deep inside, but the ones who choose to love openly will have peace and courage. Everyone is a reflection of their own heart.

You have a beautiful heart full of love. Now it is time for you to forgive and love those kids that hurt you."

Cecil squeezed her little shoulders encouragingly, and Angela looked up at his wrinkled, caring face while wiping away the last tear. She had not understood everything he had said, but something had touched her, feelings she would often reflect upon.

Cecil had many talks with Angela, as well as with Jackie and Sue Beth. He shared many concepts about life that seemed to be a contradiction to his lifestyle. But there was something about his words that presented a clear, heartfelt wisdom. The highest of highs and the lowest of lows had earned him his mentor status.

The vision of Angela returned to the luminous angel, and Cecil started walking up Third Street, half a mile to Marquette Avenue, and then east towards the porcelain company. He crossed River Road and walked along the docks and the warehouse district. He paused to look out at the Mississippi river. It was dark and foreboding as chunks of ice floated by, and a frigid wind swept across the open expanse.

He turned away, and moved into a long interconnecting alleyway. It zigzagged like an intricate maze, and it challenged his skills. He went around several more corners and noticed a group of fellow homeless gathered around a fifty-five gallon drum. A fire was blazing. A teenager, an old woman, and a couple of men were huddled around the container, soaking in the warmth. The teenager was stoking the fire with whatever he could find that would burn. Cecil was tempted to stop and warm himself, but he was too excited about the potential gifts at the Porcelain Company, and thought it best to keep moving. Then he remembered the pastries, and wanted to share. He knew he would soon be having a wonderful meal at the Macaby House. He saw them passing around a pint bottle of cheap wine. They were having their own little Christmas Eve celebration. In the glow of the flames, he held up the bag from Mulholland Bakery.

"Would you care for some fresh pastries?"

They responded enthusiastically. Looking into the bag, they selected their favorite treat and gobbled it down.

"Hey, warm yourself and have a drink," the woman said.

Cecil stepped into the circle and lifted his hands to the blaze.

"Thanks, the fire is great." He impulsively grabbed the bottle and raised it to his mouth, then stopped. He stared at the wine. The temptation was like giant claws digging into his soul and extracting his deepest resolve. He shook his head, regaining his sensibility, as he remembered the children and his commitment to them. "Thank you, but the fire will be just fine."

The heat emanated from the drum, and he absorbed as much of the reviving energy as possible. He retrieved his harmonica, held it towards the potential audience, and raised his eyebrows in question, inviting them to a front row seat at his impromptu holiday concert. Their eyes lit up, and he began playing "White Christmas." One of the men in the group, in his best attempt at a Bing Crosby voice, sang along. As the rendition concluded, the audience applauded, the performers took a slight bow, and a gentle feeling of peace lingered.

He stood there for a few moments, watching the flames and enjoying the heat. It reminded him of an unusually hot, Indian summer day when he had been busy working in the yard at the Macaby House. He enjoyed helping and was especially fond of working with the flowers. He loved to prune the rose bushes, cultivate, and weed.

He heard the back door slam, and looked up to see the children's mother, Linda, walking his way with two large glasses of lemonade. He stopped and wiped the sweat from his brow, as she handed him the tall, refreshing beverage.

"Thank you. It's much appreciated. It's a rather warm day for October," he said, as he lifted the drink to his lips and took a big gulp.

"Can we sit on the porch a minute? I'd like to talk to you."

Nodding, he sat down beside her on the swing while taking another drink.

Linda was making headway on renting a small apartment for her and the children. With help from the Macaby Foundation she was close to securing a job, and had also enrolled in a community college.

"Cecil, we'll be moving soon, and I sure hope that you'll still be the children's grandpa. I want to thank you for being there for them. It's very kind of you to spend time with them. I know they love you very much."

Cecil's voice was filled with emotion, "I love them too."

"They look to you for guidance and support." Linda continued.

"I'm not sure if I can give them much of that. A homeless man living here and there isn't much of an example."

"Cecil, they see you for what you are; a wise person who cares about them. You're their grandpa, you know. They've been through so much. But when you talk to them, they understand. It brings peace to their hearts."

"I would like to do more for them. What I understand to be true I don't always live up to. Understanding something is very different from living it," he said. "It seems that when my family died, well. . ." Emotions swelled again and he could not continue as tears filled his eyes. He swallowed hard, took off his glasses, and set them on a small table next to a flower pot. He wiped his eyes with his shirt sleeve then coughed, trying to cover up his feelings.

Linda sat quietly.

"Since the children have come into my life," he continued with difficulty, "I have felt alive for the first time in many years. They have given me a purpose for living again. They are doing much more for me than I am for them."

"It's mutual," Linda interrupted. "You're building up each other. All I know is that whatever you're doing, it really helps. Thank you for being there for them. God bless you."

"Hey, mister, are you asleep?" A voice from around the fire interrupted his thoughts.

"No. Just thinking. I must go now. Thanks for sharing your fire."

"Hey, no problem man. Thanks for the music and the donuts."

Cecil walked around several more corners, and finally reached the far end of the employee parking lot to the Porcelain Company. He made a beeline for the dumpsters.

To his delight, the garbage receptacles had been recently filled. He quickly went through the bins, trying to separate the rubbish from the treasures. Before long, he found two porcelain figurines, not perfect, but they would bring joy to the hearts of his little friends.

One of them was a knight in shining armor, sitting

upon a black stallion. In the background was an English castle. The piece was in excellent condition, except for a crack in the drawbridge leading to the castle. This was great for Jackie, when everything in his life had to be so manly. But then, in his eyes he was now the head of the house.

Another piece was perfect for Sue Beth; a forest setting with a gingerbread house and two children standing in the yard. Hansel and Gretel were nibbling on some confectionery flowers from the window box, while the witch looked on, trying to entice the children to enter her nefarious abode. Cecil wrapped the two figurines in pieces of tissue paper and placed them in cardboard boxes.

He kept digging. He was looking for the perfect gift for Angela. He dug deeper and deeper, passing by one broken item after another. He went through bin after bin. Nothing was working. Nothing was right.

At the Macaby House, everyone was busy decorating. The children were in the living room with Mrs. Macaby, placing homemade ornaments on the Christmas tree.

"Where is grandpa Cecil?" Angela asked impatiently.

"Don't worry, children. He is seldom late for the Christmas Eve celebration, but he does have a journey he has to complete first. On the twenty-fourth he has special places he must visit. It's his tradition."

"Yes, I know, " Angela said, "he has told me all about those places."

"What is a tradition?" asked Sue Beth.

"A tradition . . . hum. It is something special, an event or custom that people do over and over again, year after year," she said, as she placed another red felt heart on a high branch.

"We had a tradition when my daddy was alive," Jackie mumbled, his mouth full of crumbs. He was eating more star-shaped sugar cookies than he was hanging on the tree. "Every Christmas we would go into the forest and cut down our own tree. Sometimes we would go sledding too. That was a lot of fun."

"That's a wonderful tradition," Sarah continued, "It's one you will always want to remember. When I was a child, my whole family made homemade Christmas gifts. By the way kids, how is Cecil's present coming along? Have you finished it yet?"

Angela dropped a string of popcorn and ran into the recreation room. She pulled open a long drawer in the center of an oak desk, the place where the arts and craft materials were stored. She reached way in the back where it was hidden, pulled it out, and looked at it proudly. She dashed to the living room and handed it to Sarah.

"It's an eyeglass case! You know how grandpa Cecil is always leaving his glasses laying around, and can never find them."

Sarah looked it over. "It's beautiful kids, really beautiful. Cecil is going to love it."

"We made it out of leather and laced up the sides. Angela stamped his name right here," Sue Beth burst out with holiday excitement in her voice.

"It's lovely. Do you want to wrap it and put it under the tree? I have a little wrapping paper over there somewhere."

At the Imperial Porcelain Company, Cecil had canvassed all the bins carefully, still, nothing seemed right for Angela. Most of the figurines were broken or simply inappropriate. He was about to give up, when he noticed a smaller receptacle off to the side. It was covered with debris and barely visible. He cleared away the garbage, opened the lid, and searched through the packaging materials. There, half way down, he thought he felt an object. He pulled out more of the cardboard and paper and felt all around the container again. He finally retrieved something promising.

It was a small nativity scene. It was an open-faced, brown rock stable with little animals encircling the manger. It was also in excellent condition, except for a broken staff in a shepherd's hand. He noticed a small music box built into the bottom of the figurine. He wound the gold key several turns and the music began to play. Soft tingling sounds sent out a simple rendition of "Away in a Manger." It was ideal for

Angela. He wrapped it, and placed it with the other gifts in his backpack. Now his Christmas was complete; he had presents for the children, his journey was almost over, and his traditions were falling into place.

He lifted his face to the falling snow. "Oh, God, I thank you for this wonderful day, and for helping me find these gifts for the children."

Cecil felt a blast of cold wind sending a chill through his entire body. The temperature was dropping. He could almost measure it by degrees. His frail, old body had become a bio-thermometer, and could detect changes in barometric pressure, humidity, and temperature. The built-in weather station was telling him that it was going to be extremely cold indeed. Cecil pulled his coat tighter and braced himself against the wind. He was still far from the Macaby House but was confident that he could reach the final stop on his journey before heading for home.

Once again he moved around many corners and up tenth Avenue North to Royalston Avenue. There at the end of the street was the magnificent Harperville cathedral, a gothic-style edifice of granite and marble more than eight stories high. On the right side of the building, under snow covered pine trees, stood a life-size nativity scene. It was enclosed by a wooden fence, and straw covered the ground. A rustic stable housed statues of Mary and Joseph, watching over baby Jesus in the manger. Several shepherds looked on. Live sheep, a donkey, and a young cow nibbled on the hay. The scene was not much different from the porcelain gift Cecil had found for Angela. Each statue was incredibly realistic, and crafted in explicit detail. The scene reminded him of his years as a history teacher.

He recalled a class he had taught on famous European painters. The nativity scene was reminiscent of the painting, *'The Adoration of the Shepherds'* by Rembrandt, both in style and in the placement of the statues. The live animals, the beautiful statues, and the rustic stable created a realism that was far beyond comprehension.

♪   Cecil stood in awe as he had done many Christmases before. He moved up close to the scene and leaned on the fence. The moment became remarkably real as he looked down at the Babe in the manger.

"Hello, baby Jesus," he said reverently. "I hope you have a wonderful birthday. I hope you are warm and full, and that you feel the tender love of your parents."

He stood quietly as he reflected on his own life. He thought about the Savior and His life of sacrifices, descending to a mortal realm to help prepare the way for mankind.

The baby was wrapped in swaddling clothes. He looked vulnerable, yet majestic. The moment penetrated his soul with a profound spiritual awakening. The scene was transformed into what seemed to be an actual vision of the past.

Mary moved, picked up her infant son, and held him close to her.

"Hello, Cecil. My name is Mary and this is my husband Joseph. . ." She gestured towards the man beside her before lowering her eyes to the child in her arms,

". . .and this is Jesus." She again looked at Cecil with love and respect. "Please, Cecil, come in out of the cold. This is where we are staying for the night. This is where the child was born."

"There was no room at the inn," Joseph stated.

"Yes, I know," Cecil said. "You can come and stay at the Macaby House with me tonight, if you would like."

"Thank you, but we will be fine here," Mary said.

"We will be going home soon," Joseph reassured him.

Cecil wanted to give the child a gift, but what did he have? He reached into his pockets, hoping to find something special, a gift equal to that of the three Kings, but he had no gold, frankincense, or myrrh. From his pocket he drew the white bag containing the candy, hoping it would be an acceptable gift for the prince of peace. He held it in cupped hands, and presented it to Mary.

"This is gourmet fudge. It's worth twenty-eight dollars a pound," he said.

The baby touched Cecil's hand. "Would you like to hold the baby?" Mary asked, as she accepted the gift.

"But I can't do that. He is the Son of God, and I am just a. . ."

"A homeless man," Mary interrupted. "You feel unworthy, not deserving to embrace the Son of God?"

Cecil lowered his head.

"Listen, Cecil," Mary continued. "The day will come when my son will be without honor in his own city. He will be despised and hunted by men. He will be without money or home. His condition will be much like yours." Mary placed the baby in Cecil's arms, trusting him with her precious son.

Cecil held the child gently but securely, realizing that the fate of the world rested within his embrace.

As darkness fell upon the scene, flood lights illuminated the setting and awakened Cecil. He looked at the stable, and the images were once again statues. The event of this evening, at this place, would stay with him forever. Never before, in all the years of his journeys, had this experience been so vividly pronounced. He had gained a greater understanding of the mission of Christ and the significance of His birth. He looked over at the Babe in the manger and saw the bag of fudge laying next to His hand. He could still feel the slight weight of the baby in his arms and the overwhelming love emanating from the child.

Darkness had filled daylight, and the bitter, cold wind was consuming the emotional warmth Cecil had felt moments earlier. He carefully pulled his thin cap over his frozen ears, fearing that they might break if he pressed too hard, but the cap was of little value. As he turned from the stable, his attention was directed to the cathedral. He heard voices, angelic voices, from within. He knew he must hurry to the Macaby House but the music was so beautiful he was drawn to the sacred edifice.

Cecil opened the huge door quietly, understanding that everyone was welcome in church. He was immediately struck by the grandeur of the interior. It was decorated in gold, silver, and marble, and saints and angels were appropriately placed between the stained glass windows. On the steps leading from the nave to the main altar stood a choir of youth, about twenty in all, preparing for the midnight service. Their sweet voices emulated those of the Vienna Boy's Choir. They were singing Hallelujah from *'Christ on the Mount of Olives'* by Beethoven. The sounds sent chills down Cecil's spine.

He did not want to disturb the rehearsal nor did he want to be noticed. He sat down on a pew in the back to listen more intently, and to rest his weary legs. In the empty hall, Cecil was receiving a private performance,

♪ 7. **Concert for One** 59

and he was enjoying every minute of it.

With each beautiful hallelujah, Cecil became more and more emotional, and with each crescendo, his heart swelled in appreciation. At the end of the majestic song, forgetting where he was, he began to clap enthusiastically. The surprised choir director turned toward the unexpected noise, and the chorus sent Cecil puzzled looks.

Cecil was instantly embarrassed, when he remembered that clapping was inappropriate in this holy place. "I'm so sorry." He heard his voice echoing in the buttresses. He stood in an instant and rushed towards the door.

"Wait!" the choir director called out as he hurried after him.

Cecil thought for sure that he was in trouble; he had been asked to leave many places before. The choir director was right on his heels, as Cecil tried to push open the heavy door.

He grabbed Cecil by the arm. "Please don't go!" The words came in short, hard breaths. "My name is Father Evans. I am the choir director of this cathedral. What is your name, sir?" His smile was big and friendly.

"My name is Cecil."

"Welcome, Cecil. Please come up front so you can hear better."

Cecil moved cautiously away from the door. "Are you sure it's all right?"

"Of course, it's just fine. Let me introduce you to the Harperville Youth Choir."

Cecil nodded his head and respectfully took off his cap as he followed Father Evans up the aisle.

They approached the choir, who waited patiently. The boys and girls smiled and expressed various greetings. Some looked at each other with raised eyebrows, questioning Father Evans concern over this vagabond, while others understood his love for everyone.

"Cecil," Father Evans asked, "do you have a favorite Christmas song you would like to hear? It will be our Christmas gift to you."

Still enraptured by his experience with Mary, Joseph, and baby Jesus, Cecil asked, "Could you sing 'The Little Drummer Boy,' please?"

Without hesitation Father Evans turned, raised his arms, and with the down beat of his skilled hands, the choir began to sing "Come, they told me, Parum pum pum pum . . ."

Cecil felt blessed to have this magnificent choir singing only for him. As the song concluded, Father Evans walked over and gave Cecil a hug. Tears flowed freely.

Father Evans looked into Cecil's eyes and spoke in a whisper. "Listen, my dear friend, sometimes our destiny in life may not be fully understood, but there is great purpose in all journeys. The past is over, and tomorrow is a new day."

Cecil stood a little taller as he turned towards the choir. "Happy holidays, and thank you so much!" Then he bowed slightly, turned, and walked towards the entrance.

The choir began singing 'Silent Night' as Cecil opened the door, and he paused to listened for a moment longer. "Thank you, Father Evans," he said in a whisper. This had been a new experience for him, a welcomed addition to his Christmas journey. He hoped they would be there again next year.

The large door closed behind him.

The Macaby House was filled with excitement and laughter. Children of many sizes darted around the rooms, grateful they had a place to stay for the holidays. The recreation room was lined with several rows of tables. Each table was decorated with a candle centerpiece, proudly crafted by those spending Christmas at the Macaby House. Angela was in the kitchen stirring a bowl of juice, ice cubes, and 7-up. Sarah was busy creating a festive salad made with red and green Jell-O squares.

"Cecil is very late! He should have been here an hour ago," Angela said. "Do you think he had a problem, or maybe an accident?"

"Don't worry dear. He's been late before. Sometimes he gets sidetracked," said Sarah.

Angela wandered into the living room where their beautiful Christmas tree stood completely decorated and looking wonderful. This evening was magical, and she longed to share it with her grandpa Cecil. She trudged over to the large window facing the street. The glass was covered with condensation and cast a hazy reflection of the Christmas tree. She pulled the end of her shirt sleeve down over the palm of her hand, rubbed a circle in the center of the window, and scanned the street hopefully. There was no one in sight, only blowing snow and dark, ominous clouds, sweeping across a dim, somber moon.

Angela returned to the kitchen, looking discouraged and reflective.

"Mrs. Macaby, why did Cecil become a homeless man?"

"People become homeless for many different reasons, and in Cecil's case it was due to a tragedy. Many years ago, when he was a young man, he was married and had two children, twins, a girl and a boy. They were a little younger than you are now. I think their names were Jessie and Justin, or something like that."

Angela sat down at the table and rested her chin on the back of her hands.

"Cecil was a professor at a prominent university," she continued, "a teacher of history. He was promoted to dean of his department, which is highly unusual for a young man. At a party in his honor, he was given a new car. When he and his wife, Catherine, arrived home, they awakened the children and took them for a ride. Everyone was excited."

Angela was giving Mrs. Macaby her undivided attention, staring at her with large eyes.

"They were cruising down the road, listening to the radio, and Cecil was explaining some of the special features of the car. He looked down at the radio dial, then looked up, and saw a large deer in the middle of the road. He hit the breaks hard, but there was not enough time to stop. Cecil turned sharply, but the car hit the back end of the animal, and the car spun on the ice. They went off the road and down the embankment into the river. He escaped from the vehicle, but his family was drowned."

"You mean his whole family died? That's really sad." Angela said as tears filled her eyes.

"He feels that if he had been more careful and had tried harder, his family would be alive today." Sarah continued. "He has never forgiven himself. Something snapped inside him, and he lost his motivation. I think his homeless condition is the way he subconsciously punishes himself," she said, then realized that her comments were maybe too complicated for Angela. "Now, the reason he keeps going is because of friends like you and Sue Beth and Jackie. You kids have brought new life to his soul, but he still has a long way to go. He doesn't like to talk about it. He doesn't want to remember, but he can't forget. I know that he has dreams. You know, nightmares. They really hurt him."

"But it wasn't his fault! It was an accident," Angela stated.

"We know that. But Cecil is the one who has to understand."

At that moment the front door opened. A gust of wind blew all the way to the kitchen, and Angela jumped up.

"Cecil! It's Cecil!" she cried, and ran to the front room to greet him, but standing in the entrance was

Pete Webster, the maintenance man.

"I thought you were Cecil," she said with obvious disappointment.

"Sorry about that. I'm sure he'll be coming home soon."

The old-fashioned, mercury thermometer on Jensen's drugstore seemed to scream out in pain as the temperature dropped with arctic harshness. The darkness intensified the beauty of the Christmas lights everywhere, flickering in the snow and flurry. The streets were void of shoppers and carolers as the temperature fell to five degrees.

Cecil pressed on. He had finished his Christmas journey and had picked up a few new traditions on the way. Having fed his soul, his only goal now was to make it to the Macaby House. He knew it was late and that the children would be worried.

As he walked by a small gift shop, he noticed a variety of games on display. A Scrabble game was open and set up with letters artistically placed on the board. The letters spelled out the words 'Merry Christmas.' As he walked on, he reflected on a day several months earlier, when he and the children had been playing the game.

"It is too a word. M-I-F-E-L spells Mifel," Sue Beth stated enthusiastically.

"What does it mean?" Jackie queried.

"It means. . . it means. . . I don't know what it means, but it means something."

"There is no such word," Angela declared, "It's not here in the dictionary."

"Okay, smarty pants," said Sue Beth, as she looked over her letters again, "then I have another word. D-E-A-T-H, death!"

"Yes, that's a good word," Cecil said. "You get 16 points for that one. You have a triple letter score for the H."

Angela looked up at Cecil. Her demeanor changed dramatically, as she spoke out in a serious tone. "Death. What does that mean? Our daddy died. Where is he? Is he in heaven, or is he just dead?"

Cecil paused. He was used to Angela's precocious questions, but this one caught him off guard. He started slowly, pulling his chair closer to the children. "We know that everyone is born and that everyone dies, don't we? Some people live on the earth for a short time, and some live much longer."

"Like you, grandpa Cecil. You've lived a long, long time. You're very old, aren't you?" Jackie stated.

"Yes, Jackie, I am," Cecil chuckled.

"I don't want to die," Sue Beth said, contemplating her destiny.

"In the Bible it says that after death we will all live again," Cecil continued.

"Does that mean in heaven?" Angela asked.

"Some people call it that," Cecil answered. "It is a place where we continue to live on."

"Is that where our daddy is?" Angela asked.

"I believe he is. I really do."

They sat quietly for a moment, then Cecil, hoping to put it all into perspective, asked, "Do you know what a legacy is?"

The children glanced at each other with puzzled looks.

"A legacy is what you leave behind when you die. It is the good or the bad in our lives for which we are remembered. Jesus taught that after death, we live again. We go on to the next world. Your father's time on earth is over, but he left you children a legacy, the legacy of his good name."

"He was a good dad," Angela interrupted. "He really did love us."

"Now it's up to each of you," Cecil continued, "to honor your name and your father's name. You will carry on this legacy, and then someday your children will carry on yours. There is a song which says that when we die and are gone, another child will be born to carry on. . . that is what life and death is about, one continuous circle." Cecil paused and drew a large circle in the air. "Carrying on the legacy. That is why death should be a happy time, a rejoicing in what a person has accomplished in life, and a celebration of the life to come.

"That's hard to understand," said Jackie.

"I'm sure it is," said Cecil, "but don't worry about it now. Someday you will understand."

"I understood it all," said Angela.

"You always think you're so smart!" Jackie said. "Your liguicy will be the pain you caused your brother."

"It's legacy," Angela corrected.

"Remember what I said about the love you show towards yourself and others," Cecil reminded them. "That is also important in life."

"I suppose," Angela said, "but little brothers don't make it easy."

Cecil wondered if his ideas were of any help to the children. He was not able to reason out his own destiny, so what business did he have to try and help anyone else? He hoped they would be smarter than he was.

Cecil slowed to catch his breath in front of the Manning Arms Hotel, one of the city's most prestigious establishments. Limousines, Cadillacs, Rolls-Royces, and other fine vehicles pulled in front of the elegant building. The city's rich and famous, clad in formal attire, came and went as they attended the most celebrated holiday parties in town.

As Cecil crossed the red carpet leading into the hotel, he stopped. He felt the periodic warmth coming from inside, when the automatic doors opened and closed.

The people moved around Cecil. Some carried expressions of disgust, while others were indifferent. A stately gentleman, in a black tuxedo and long overcoat, approached Cecil in a cheerful manner.

"Happy holidays. How are you this evening?"

"Just fine, thank you. Kind of cold. I'm trying to make it to the Macaby House before the storm gets worse."

♪ The man grabbed Cecil's hand and shook it respectfully. "Merry Christmas," he said, as he turned and walked into the hotel. Cecil felt something in his hand and looked down to see a twenty dollar bill. He was not one to beg for money, or for anything else for that matter, but he wasn't beyond accepting a kind gesture.

The captain of the bellhops glared at Cecil. He

marched out and stated, "Old man, you need to move on. Quit bothering our patrons! We get tired of you bums hanging out and begging for money!"

Cecil left, tucking the money into his pocket. He was pleased by the generous gift he had received. As he turned the corner, three young men in their late teens stopped him abruptly.

"Give me the money, old man."

A shorter boy, wearing a red bandanna around his head, gave Cecil a push.

"We saw the rich dude, man. The one who put the money in your hand. Now, give it to me."

Another boy grabbed his arm, twisting it behind him.

The shorter boy gave Cecil another shove, this time with greater force.

Cecil reached into his coat pocket, willing to give up his newly acquired fortune.

About half a block away, there were two officers on patrol. They were parked by a fire hydrant finishing their Christmas Eve dinner: Arby's roast beef sandwiches, hot pies, and cocoa. They would naturally prefer being home with their families, but someone had to work, even on Christmas Eve.

As officer Johnson took another bite of his sandwich, he noticed the three boys and Cecil. He watched, as the middle kid became aggressive.

"Banelli, look over there. Looks like some gang

members are harassing that ol' man."

Most of the police have little tolerance for the indigent. But the gangs prey on everyone, especially the homeless.

Officer Johnson hit the siren and lights and swung into the street, heading for the boys and Cecil. They pulled up to the curb and jumped out. As soon as the boys saw the police car, they were off and running.

"Are you al' right?" Officer Johnson asked.

"Yes, sir, I'm fine. And I still have my money."

"Old man, it's cold out here, and it's getting colder," Banelli said. "Where're you staying tonight?"

"The Macaby House."

"That's far away, man."

Banelli leaned over to Johnson and said discretely, "Should we give 'em a ride?"

"Sure. It's Christmas 'n' all, you know."

"You wan' a ride?" Banelli asked.

"To jail. . .?"

The officers looked at each other and smiled.

"No, to the Macaby House."

"Oh! That would be wonderful."

Johnson opened the back door and Cecil started to board. Right then, a call came over the radio.

"A robbery of business in progress at the Quick Mart convenience store, Grant and Willow," the dispatcher announced.

"Sorry," Banelli expressed. "But we have to respond

to this robbery."

They jumped in the car, and with sirens blaring and lights flashing, they headed toward the crime-scene.

Disappointed, Cecil pushed along again. The blizzard, the extreme cold, and his poor eyesight made it difficult to move and see. An hour later his energy was nearly gone. His steps were slow and lumbering, and he realized that he would never reach the Macaby House on foot.

"The twenty-dollars!" he suddenly remembered.

He looked up and down the avenue, searching for a taxi. He gestured and waved at several passing cabs to no avail. The homeless and indigent were not considered good fare prospects. One driver looked in Cecil's direction but kept on driving. Finally, a yellow cab pulled up to the curb. Cecil opened the door, and began to enter, excited about the ride.

"Where are you going," the driver asked.

"The Macaby House."

"You mean that homeless place? I don't think so," he said as he spun out and headed down the road.

"But wait! I have money!" Cecil yelled, as he waived his twenty dollar bill.

Everyone at the Macaby House was enjoying the festivities of the evening, except for Angela.

"Why don't you prepare a plate of treats for Cecil and put it in the fridge?" her mother suggested.

"Yes, I guess I better. But it's not the same as having

him here."

Angela took great care in arranging the cookies, candies, and cheesecake on the plate. When she was finished, she wrapped it in aluminum foil and carefully set it in the refrigerator next to his dinner plate.

"Mom, I want to go and look for Cecil right now. I'm sure we can find him."

"I know you children are concerned. I am too. But there is a storm brewing out there, and we don't know which direction he will be coming from. Maybe he had to find another place to stay for the night. It's very late, you know. Talking about late, you kids should be in bed."

"Well, I'm going to stay on the couch so I can be close to the phone. Maybe he'll call," Angela said with resolve.

Cecil stood at a corner pay phone. He desperately needed help, and the people at the Macaby House were the only ones he knew that could come to his rescue. A small handful of pennies, nickels, dimes, and one quarter had been bestowed upon him by a last-minute shopper earlier in the day. He would use some of it on a phone call. His hands were shaking terribly, and some of the money slipped through his fingers. He squatted and picked up a couple of coins. With stiff, numb fingers, he searched through the powdery snow for the rest of the buried coins. He found the thirty-five cents he needed for the call, and stood. He could find the rest in a minute.

His fingers were so frozen, he had a difficult time inserting the coins into the slot, but finally managed. Six, three, seven. . . what was the number after seven? He reached for the phone directory, and fumbled through the few pages that were left in the book. The M's and many other sections had been torn out, as were most of the Yellow Pages.

Cecil knew he had to move on, but first he had to find the rest of the coins. There was maybe forty or fifty cents buried in the snow, and a homeless man, even in extreme circumstances, would never leave money behind. He bent down to retrieve the assorted coins that lay in the snow beneath his feet. As he struggled to grasp them, he noticed a bus token. Why had he not thought of the bus before? But would he have enough time? He knew that they were only in service until one o'clock in this part of town.

He looked up and down the avenue, searching for a clock. About halfway down the next block was Citizen's National Bank. The clock was too far away to see the numbers clearly. He pulled out his glasses and wiped them on his shirt-tail. Putting them on, he moved forward, raised his head, and squinted. The digital sign on the bank brought news of hope and despair. The time read twelve forty-two, the temperature read seven degrees below. Could he make it in time?

He stood on a street with no bus route and navigated mentally, remembering that there was a bus stop every block or so along most main streets. He looked again at the token, then held it tightly. He moved along with renewed hope of making it to the Macaby House and the children. With this faith his spirits lifted and his physical endurance revived.

About half a block down the road he came to a stairway that led to a lower level street. He paused and looked down the long, steep stairs. He took a deep breath, and the air entered his lungs with a sharp, cold pain. A bus was approaching.

He descended the cobblestone steps, grabbing the railing for support, one calculated step after another. Suddenly, a tear in the sole of his boot became wedged in a broken stone. His body gyrated, throwing his head against the rough concrete wall with a hard thump. He tried to regain his footing, and staggered, holding onto the rail tightly. He was half standing, and half sitting.

His face had a deep scrape above the right eyebrow, and a bump to complement it. Blood oozed from the abrasion, but the freezing cold provided nature's perfect remedy, as the crimson droplets instantly froze. He was dizzy, somewhat confused, and his vision was blurred. He could hear the bus coming closer, and was alert enough to know that if he missed this opportunity, there would be no other.

The bus came to a halt, as his foot hit the bottom

step. The door flew open, and Cecil forced his body across the sidewalk and onto the bus, struggling to drop the token into the fare box. He slumped onto the nearest seat. A few stops down the line, and he would be within two blocks of his destination.

For now he rested, taking in what little heat the bus had to offer. The thumping of the tires hitting the road formed a rhythmic accompaniment to Christmas carols that seemed to indiscriminately bounce around in his head. He stared out the window on the opposite side. Blurry stretches of lights, trees, and buildings passed by in monotony.

On the wall of the bus, above the doors and windows, were company advertisements promoting everything from cars to milk. One in particular caught his attention. The message, at least in his mind, screamed out in condemnation. The sign read, "Manhattan Mutual Life: Prepare for Your Family's Future."

"The past, the present, the future, the yesterdays, and the tomorrow's. . . what did I give my family?" he thought.

Question after question arose in his mind. "Of what did I deprive my children? Education? Marriage? Yes, but also all of the other great possibilities life has to offer. And my dear Catherine," he continued, "I took her youth, her children, and the love we shared. I took it all. . . ," he sighed, " . . . from them and myself."

These guilt trips were common, but on this cold Christmas morning, within his deprived condition, the guilt and pain were so much more pronounced.

The bus had made four stops. He knew that the next one would put him at Lyndale Avenue, and close to home. As the bus slowed down, he glanced up at the street sign. It read "First Street." A scared, sick feeling stirred in his stomach as he realized he had gone the wrong way. He had boarded a bus going in the opposite direction, and was now miles farther from his destination. There was no time to take another bus back, and he wasn't familiar with this part of the city.

He exited the bus and trembled with fear, feeling defeated. The Macaby House seemed beyond his reach, and never finding peace regarding his family filled him with hopelessness. He dragged his feet along, as the agony grew with each step.

He yelled at the roaring wind in indignation, "Prepare for your family's future? What future? They don't have a future! They are dead . . . I killed them."

Cecil leaned against a lamp post in surrender. Everything seemed impossible; he had no reason to go on. He wrapped his arms around his head, and sobbed. Heavy with emotion, his legs buckled. He grabbed the post, hugged it tightly, and continued to cry. He gradually slipped down the post to his knees.

A few vehicles passed by, their headlights shined on a store front window across the sidewalk from Cecil. The glare caught his attention, and through tear filled eyes, he saw his distorted image in the glass. He stared at his face in contempt.

Whirling snow began to dance on the window, creating shapes that gradually transformed into a multitude of faces. People throughout his life who had rejected him, who had treated him with prejudice and hate, people who had offended him in so many ways. Among the images where the Rankin's security guard, the Manning Arms bellhop, and the gang members. He heard their voices again; "Give me your money, old man." "You don't want to spend the night in jail, do you?" "We get tired of you bums bothering our patrons." The voices became harsh and overpowering. Then gradually, he heard other voices; kind and gentle voices. Many were seeking his love and forgiveness. He looked into their eyes and felt their remorse. As each voice continued to plea, Cecil was overcome with compassion, and realized that it was time. He felt a great burden lift as he reached out with forgiveness.

Soon the whirling snow gathered the faces and carried them away, leaving only one image, the one other person he needed to forgive, the wrinkled old man in the center of the window pane. For the first time, he realized that he could forgive everyone, and everyone included himself. The cords of guilt that bound him could be broken, if not today, then tomorrow. With this understanding, his physical plight did not seem so foreboding. He had hope again, and with hope, anything is possible.

He adjusted his cap and gloves, pulled his ragged scarf tighter around his neck, and from somewhere deep inside, he summoned the determination and courage of an Arctic explorer. He would go on with fortitude and conviction, and he would not stop until he reached the Macaby House and the people he loved.

Cecil walked for more than two hours.

"Oh, God, give me the strength to go on!" The prayer fell from his lips many times. His legs continued to move, even when he had nothing left to give.

He finally saw some life in this dead part of the city. He approached a house with a TV flickering in the background. He knocked several times. A heavyset man, wearing a tank-top and boxer shorts, pulled the curtain partly open and looked out at the scruffy, old vagrant on his doorstep. Cecil only needed directions, but the man didn't want anyone interfering with his holiday television.

He waved Cecil off, "Get out of here you bum!"

The wind was blowing even harder, setting the snow into furious commotion. He paused, looked all around him, and realized that he was completely disoriented and lost. Nothing was familiar.

He needed help desperately, but there was no one to be found. The streets were bare in all directions. He tried to be positive, but moments of hopelessness sunk deep into his soul. All he needed was a familiar landmark; a building or a sign, something that could set him on the right path.

He dragged himself along for about another two blocks, when something caught his attention. Off to his right was a narrow walkway which led to a flashing, red neon sign. He strained to look down the semi-dark path where he saw a lighted window and a door at the end. The neon sign was written in an oriental script and he immediately assumed that it was some sort of an Asian restaurant, or maybe a Chinese tailor.

As Cecil shuffled closer, the red light illuminated the snow around him, giving off an artificial presence of warmth. Galvanized garbage cans lined the wall, and halfway down the alley, one can was tipped over, most likely by an animal or a homeless person in search of food. Bits and pieces of oriental vegetables and meat lay in the snow.

Arriving at the door, he noticed another sign, a small one. TOKYO RESTAURANT, DELIVERIES ONLY BETWEEN 10AM AND 4PM. Cecil tried the door but it was locked. He tried to look through the window to his right but it was too far away from the steps. Several card-board boxes blocked his ability to position himself under the window, so he kicked the boxes to free them from the crusted snow and ice that held them securely in place. Soon he stood under the window, and by standing on a wooden crate, he could peer into the lowest corner pane. The frost covered the entire surface, and he struggled to look inside. He wiped hard with his gloved hands, and the frost gradually scraped away. He strained to see. An elderly, Asian man was mopping the floor. Excited and hopeful, Cecil knocked on the window. The prospect of warmth and help thrilled him. He knocked harder, but the old man didn't respond. Then Cecil noticed that he was wearing a Walkman. Cecil began to wave with both hands, hoping to draw his attention. Instead, the man moved further from the window as he continued to mop, disappearing into the back. In desperation, Cecil picked up a chunk of broken cement and was ready to smash the window, when the old man returned and noticed Cecil's movement.

The man stepped closer to the window and looked out suspiciously. He spoke in broken English, "We no open."

With desperation in his voice, Cecil pleaded, "Please don't go. I need help. I need directions. Can you please help me?"

The old man looked confused, but surveyed Cecil's situation, and opened the door. Through the screened door, which was locked, Cecil asked politely, but with a tone of urgency, "Do you know where the Macaby House is?"

"Eigo wo wakarimasen," said the man.

"Macaby House," Cecil repeated again slowly.

After a few moments of glancing at the floor, and

then the ceiling, the old man nodded, and replied with Japanese pronunciation, "Makabi Hasu, Hai wakari-masu."

Unknown to Cecil, the Tokyo restaurant had donated food to the shelter on special occasions. Cecil could see that the man understood as he pointed north westerly. Then grabbing a napkin, and taking a pen from behind his ear, he sketched out a crude map.

The mop was flopping in the air as he gestured again, "kita nishi no ho."

The old fellow looked down at Cecil and understood his deprived and depleted condition. Having lived in Japan most of his life, including World War II, the old man was profoundly aware of hardship and suffering.

"Dozo haite, haite," he said with a toothless smile, as he stepped aside to let Cecil enter.

The restaurant was so warm on Cecil's frozen face and hands that after a few moments they started stinging. The man offered Cecil a chair and table next to a small, Japanese style heater. Cecil struggled to the table, taking hold of the chair for support. He labored to bend his frozen, almost paralyzed limbs. He was still feeling dizzy.

"Chottomatte ne," the old man said, as he dashed off to the kitchen, returning quickly with a cup of rice and a bowl of Miso, a Japanese soup made from bean curd and tofu. He then placed a hot, white washcloth that was resting in a bamboo, boat-like holder, in front of Cecil. The old man motioned for Cecil to wash off his hands and face.

Cecil unfolded the hot cloth, and placed it on his cold face. He could feel the heat soaking into every pore. Next, he placed it on the bloody abrasion and bump, wiping them clean.

"Thank you so much," Cecil expressed, as he lifted the bowl to his mouth and sipped the delicious soup. He thought that never in his life had food tasted so good as this hot, wonderful soup and tender sticky-rice. It was indeed manna from heaven.

♪ Pointing to his nose and grinning, the old man said, "Me, Tanaka."

Cecil, without thinking, responded likewise, "Me, Cecil."

Tanaka bowed, and Cecil returned the courtesy, almost hitting his head on the table.

Tanaka glanced over at Cecil as he ate his welcomed Christmas meal. "Samui desu ne," he said, as he hugged his body and shivered.

"Oh, yes," Cecil replied, understanding his gesture, "and I have felt every bit of it."

Shaking the bowl to gather even the smallest bits of tofu, Cecil swallowed down the last mouthful of soup and rice. He stood, pulled the last few coins from his pocket, and offered to pay.

Tanaka shook his head in resistance, "My Merry

Christmas gift."

Cecil looked at Mr. Tanaka. Not so long ago, as a Corporal in the Philippine Islands, he was at war with these people, maybe Tanaka himself. But the wounds of times past were healed, and they were simply two people sharing in the spirit of Christmas. He thought how easy it was to forgive others, and so difficult to forgive oneself.

Cecil, with one of the five Japanese words in his vocabulary, thanked him, "Arigato!" reached out, and gave him a warm and grateful hand shake.

Making sure Cecil had the napkin, Tanaka pointed one more time to the North-West. He bowed respectfully, and Cecil returned the gesture.

With renewed energy and directions, Cecil felt confident that he could now find his way. He was ready to venture again.

CHRISTMAS MORNING, 3:22 A.M.

Cecil moved along for half an hour or so, trying to follow Tanaka's map. The wind was blowing harder, increasing in velocity by the minute. He held tightly to the map, trying to read the directions as he walked. Suddenly, a gust of wind caught the napkin, sending it spinning into the air. He watched his hope disappear out of sight.

Cecil looked around in all directions, and realized that he was lost. He could go on no further. He needed shelter. He would have to find the Macaby House in the morning when it was light, and wait to be with the children on Christmas day. Frustrated again, he turned into an alley in the back of some tall buildings. They provided partial relief from the weather, and he took a seat on a sheltered, concrete slab. He was totally exhausted. The elements had taken their toll, and it felt good to rest his back against the brick wall.

Cecil tried hard to keep warm, but his whole body was shaking, and his limbs were stiffening again.

A dingy-looking alley cat poked his head around the corner. "Well, Merry Christmas to you, mister cat. Looks like we're both lost souls tonight. I'm trying to find the Macaby House. Do you know where it is?" The cat wandered over to Cecil and rubbed against his legs.

Cecil put his hands in his coat pockets, looking for

warmth, and felt a piece of the fudge that had fallen out of the bag. He put the candy in his mouth, letting the creamy confection melt on his tongue. He recalled the beautiful young lady at Rankin who had been so kind to him, and the gourmet fudge that had made such a fine gift for the Babe. He reflected for a few moments about the special events of the day; the pastries from the Mulholland Bakery, finding the gifts for the children, and the beautiful voices of the Harperville choir.

Cecil reached over and stroked the cat's head. "I'm going to make a bed over here in the corner, mister cat, and you are welcome to share it if you like."

But the cat had found a piece of frozen ham in the snow, and as soon as it was devoured, he moved on in search of better pickings. Cecil knew he needed to make his shelter quickly. Even colder weather was yet to come. He pushed several smaller garbage cans into a semi circle, then opened the lid of a larger container, and pulled out a few crushed cardboard boxes, some packing material, and a bundle of newspapers. He proceeded to create a mattress, and saved plenty of newspapers for his blanket. He climbed into his bed, making it as comfortable as possible.

Then, half asleep, he thought of something, and struggled to sit up. He searched his pockets for something to write with, and finally found a little stub of a pencil. He took the porcelain gifts from his backpack, and with a shaking hand, he slowly wrote on the side of the gifts: Jackie, Sue Beth, and Angela, in care of the Macaby House.

He lay his head on some wadded up newspaper, placed the gifts next to him, then took Angela's gift of baby Jesus from its box. He stared at the holy scene, as the street lights and blowing snow fell upon the small manger. He wound the key several turns, and listened as the roaring wind reached out like eagle's claws, tearing away its musical prey.

"Good night, children. Good night, baby Jesus," he said, feeling the true spirit of the occasion.

His exhausted and diminished body fell sound asleep, as the temperature fell to twelve degrees below zero.

He dreamed. Visions of the past, in varied degrees of plainness and distortion, darted around within his slumber. The same nightmare he had had so many times before returned with increased intensity.

He and his family were in the new car. The deer bounced onto the road, the car swerved, tumbled down the embankment, and plunged into the river. He yelled to his family, "Get out! Get out!" Frantically, he rolled down the window and escaped.

Cecil's face became twisted within his sleep as he became progressively agitated. He saw himself breaking the water's surface, treading water and ice, and watching the car quickly disappearing. The pleadings and screams from his family were cutting deep, as he desperately dove into the river again and again. He tried with all his might to rescue them, but it was hopeless. The water was too muddy, and the night too dark.

Cecil awakened with a start. His frozen, numb body felt little as the frigid cold blew through his humble shelter. His attention was drawn to a brick wall across the alley. The old stones, in varied shades of red, brown, and white, were dusted in snow. Some were cracked and chipped, reflecting a rustic, urban beauty created by the elements and neglect. As he stared at the wall, the surface began to change. The bricks became smooth and clean, and the multicolored surface blended into a soft, shiny white. Not bright or harsh, but warm and inviting.

The glow created peace. Cecil felt no cold or pain, and he wasn't sure if he was awake or dreaming. He laid still and watched. From within the light he saw abstract, flowing images, moving and changing into nondescript forms that gradually became human in shape and nature.

♪   Standing before him were his wife, Catherine, and his twins, Jessie and Justin. They had not aged a day from the time of the accident.

The twins spoke out almost in unison, "Hi daddy. We've missed you."

When the children looked at their father, they saw

him as the young, vibrant man he had been in the past. The children ran over to him and embraced him tightly. As he bent over to meet their size, he looked into their faces, visually caressing every feature.

"We've missed you, daddy," Jessie's voice cracked as she whispered. "We love you, daddy."

"I love you too. But is this real?" he asked, as he hugged them again and again.

"Hello, Cecil. It's been a long time. We've all missed you so much," Catherine walked up to Cecil and embraced him. They held each other for a long time, as tears mutually flowed. She also recognized him as a young man.

"We've come, the children and I, to tell you something. Something you should have realized a long time ago."

The children watched intently, as their mother expressed their mutual convictions.

Catherine was compassionate but firm. "Ever since that night so long ago, that night the deer ran into the highway, you have tortured yourself with the idea that you either caused or could have prevented the accident. But that is exactly what it was; an accident, and nothing more. Life is full of experiences that we have little or no control over. Sometimes things just happen."

Cecil listened intently. He wanted to believe every word, but the years of guilt and blame were difficult to surrender. Catherine looked deep into Cecil's eyes again, embraced him, and kissed him.

"Daddy, it wasn't your fault." said Jessie.

"But why have you waited so long to come to me?" Cecil asked.

"You would never let us come before now," Justin said.

"We've tried to come to you many times, but your heart was not ready." The compassion in Catherine's eyes gave Cecil a hope he had never before experienced.

"But why now?" he asked, wanting to believe; wanting release from the pain.

"Because of the changes in your life, and the children," Catherine expressed. "Sue Beth, Jackie, and Angela. Especially Angela. They have taught you to open your heart. You have learned how to love again, and we needed that link between us, so you could stop resisting our presence."

They held each other again.

"We must go now," Catherine whispered.

"Will I see you and the children again?"

"Yes, you will. We are with you now, tomorrow, and forever. Cecil, let it go. It was not your fault. You have to forgive yourself." With that statement, she and the children faded back into the light and the wall.

Cecil was back in his makeshift bed, looking at the brick wall with no lights and no images remaining.

Had it been a dream? A vision? Or was it the depleted, delusionary condition of a man overcome by age and elements?

He lay in deep thought, pondering the events of the evening. The words of his dear wife and children penetrated his soul with profound clarity and conviction. He hoped that Catherine's words would be a reality, and someday, somewhere, they would be together again.

For the first time in over forty years, Cecil fell asleep at peace with himself and his family. His pain was gone. Their love embraced him.

♪   The morning was calm and the sun shone brightly on the satin, white snow. The faint sounds of church bells welcomed in the Christmas morning. The air was crisp and cold, and a blanket of snow covered Cecil as he lay quietly. A slight wind blew across his bed, and removed some of the snow, exposing his arm and boot. Cecil's friend, the alley cat, returned and rubbed against his hand.

"Are you dead, mister?" The young boy's voice echoed from the past, but this time, there was no movement and no rumbling from beneath the cardboard bed. The boy's prophetic words had been fulfilled. During the night, Cecil had died. He had died in a freezing, peaceful slumber in the alley behind the Macaby House.

A siren approached from a distance, disrupting the silence of the sacred morning. The noise startled Angela as it came closer, and she jumped from the couch, still clutching Cecil's gift.

The city ambulance zoomed around the corner and jerked to a stop at the end of the alley. Angela was first out the back door, but Jackie and Sue Beth were close behind.

In shock Angela looked on from a distance, praying that her worst fear was not before her, as the paramedics checked the man's vital signs. But something deep down inside told her that the man being placed on the gurney was Cecil, and he was dead. The paramedics adjusted the body and covered it with a sheet.

The flashing red and blue lights reflecting on the snow created a festive Christmas atmosphere in stark contrast to the tragedy before them. The paramedics wheeled the gurney towards the ambulance as the Macaby House residents and other neighbors gathered around the scene. A police car had arrived and officers were keeping the public at a distance.

Sarah grabbed Linda's hand. "The children are going to be so hurt," she said, not wanting to believe what she was seeing.

Angela took the lead, grabbed Jackie and Sue Beth by the hand, and walked closer. They maneuvered between some spectators, as they headed for the ambulance and the approaching gurney. Linda noticed the children, and wanted to stop them, but hesitated, she knew that they needed to say goodbye to their dear friend.

A police officer stepped in behind the children. "Hold it!" he shouted, "don't go over there."

The gurney was brought to an abrupt stop. "Kids, please move out of the way," a paramedic insisted. The officer and the paramedics towered over the children with impatience and frustration. They tried to push on through the adolescent roadblock, but the children did not move.

Angela looked up at the paramedics. "Excuse us, please. This man is our friend, and our grandpa, and we would like to say goodbye."

The paramedics glanced at each other, touched by this little girl's sincerity. They looked at the police officer with an expression that asked, "What shall we do?"

The officer paused for a moment, wondering how this black man could possibly be the grandfather of three white children, but he also sensed that there was some type of attachment.

He turned to Angela, and spoke formally, "Okay, you can have a minute."

The paramedics lowered the gurney to the children's level. Angela stepped up, and pulled the sheet from Cecil's face. His skin was chalky white. Jackie and Sue Beth began to cry. Angela turned toward them.

"Please, don't cry. This is not a time to be sad. We are here to say goodbye, and to wish Cecil a Merry Christmas." She turned back to Cecil. "Grandpa Cecil, we brought your Christmas gift. Sue Beth, Jackie, and I made it for you. It's for your glasses. You know how you're always losing them." She looked around for his glasses, then asked the paramedics, "Do you have Cecil's glasses?"

The female attendant reached in her medical bag, retrieved the glasses, and handed them to Angela.

Angela put the glasses in the case, and placed it in his shirt pocket, next to his harmonica. "Now there, you will never lose your glasses again," she said. She looked down at Cecil one last time, touched his cheek, and kissed his forehead. "Goodbye, Grandpa Cecil." She replaced the sheet. "You may go now," she said to the paramedics.

A tender smile stole across the female attendants face. "I saw three boxes over there where we found. . . your friend. I think they might be for you."

The paramedics loaded the gurney and drove away. Angela had not shed a tear. She knew better, but it was difficult for Sue Beth and Jackie to hold them back.

The crowd disbursed quickly. A dead indigent was not worth much attention, except to those who knew and loved him.

The children walked down the alleyway to Cecil's shelter. The names on the boxes were scribbled but legible. They traded one with another, and each received their gift, except Angela's box was empty. She stooped, and rummaged through the debris.

Jackie pulled out the knight on the horse, and felt Cecil's trust in him. He hoped that he could be as brave as the knight that was seated on the powerful horse.

Sue Beth examined the colorful gingerbread house and the two little children standing in the front. "How lost they look," she whispered, feeling as lost as they. What a treasure this gift was to her.

Angela found her gift, and what a perfect gift it was on this beautiful Christmas morning. She looked at the scene before her with reverence and appreciation. As she studied it closer, the music began to play.

Jackie and Sue Beth could no longer hold back the tears, and let them flow freely.

"Why did he have to die?" Jackie questioned. "He was so good to us. And he loved us. We need him!"

"But he's gone," Sue Beth said, "and we'll never see him again."

Angela interrupted. "But that's not true. Don't you remember what he taught us? What he shared with us about life and love and death. Don't you remember?"

Then Jackie and Sue Beth, as if receiving a revelation, began to smile, and Angela smiled back.

They started walking back to the Macaby House, thinking about the many lessons that Cecil had taught them. Then, once again they heard his voice within their hearts. It was a voice that penetrated every fiber of their being.

"My dear children, keep me close to you. Remember what we shared, and let that be my legacy to you. Children, be happy. Be the best you can be. Remember that the greatest gift we can give to mankind is love. Live the spirit of Christmas every day. Feed the hungry, bless the poor, and heal the sick. Reach out to everyone in need, sometimes giving, and sometimes receiving, but most importantly, always loving."

They held their treasured gifts tightly. Each child had the seeds of Cecil's love and wisdom growing within them. They would embrace his words many times throughout their lives.

Suddenly, the children stopped and turned. Their attention was drawn to that special section of the brick wall in the alley. They could hear soft strains of Cecil's harmonica. They sensed that he was with his family, he was home, and that someday they would also be with their father again.

Angela began to cry. Not tears of sadness, but of joy, for she knew that Cecil was now complete and happy, ♪ and for that understanding, so was she.

FORREST B. PETERSON is a professional writer, theatrical producer, and teacher. He studied marketing and writing at Eastern New Mexico and Idaho State universities, as well as film production at Metro Media Productions in Florida. He has written over fifty stage plays, movie scripts, short stories, and a novel. His film, Trouble in Oz, won five Crystal Reel Awards from the Florida Film Festival in 1990. He teaches marketing, drama, and film production. He is married to Carol Ralston, and they have five children.

VICTORIA E. KING grew up in Oslo, Norway, and moved to the States in 1980 where she began her education at BYU, Idaho. She studied fine arts and graphic design between raising five children, and has managed her own graphic design business for the past nine years. She has also taught classical ballet for fifteen years, produced a variety of dance recitals, and performed as a dancer. She enjoys painting and sculpting, but her greatest interest is portrait drawing. As a single mother, she loves the opportunity to work at home.